If Kids Could Ask the President One Question...

"Children should be seen, not heard."

—V.W. Bellamy in
Table Rules for Little Folks

If Kids Could Ask the President One Question...

Over 100 Children's Essays
Written for the SCHOLASTIC NEWS
Journalism Awards Contest

Selected by the Editors of
SCHOLASTIC NEWS

SCHOLASTIC INC.
New York Toronto London Auckland Sydney Tokyo

Acknowledgments

Much appreciation to the SCHOLASTIC NEWS staff for their time and thoughtful concern in reading and judging the 32,000 entries.

Praise for the teachers and parents across the U.S. who encouraged the children and made it all possible.

Special thanks to Martha Pichey who played a major role in coordinating this project.

Thank you's to Art Buchwald, Pam Dawber, Tomie dePaola, Lee Bennett Hopkins, Caroline Kennedy, and Shari Lewis for their sound judgments in helping us choose the winners.

Finally, the greatest thanks to each of the children who shared their powerful ideas and taught us so much.

Library of Congress Cataloging in Publication Data
Main entry under title:

If kids could ask the president one question—.

1. Children—United States—Attitudes. 2. Children—Political activity—United States.
3. Presidential candidates—United States. 4. Children's writings.
I. Scholastic news.
HQ792.U513   1984   305.2'3   84-10922
ISBN 0-590-33469-7

12 11 10 9 8 7 6 5 4 3 2 1   8   4 5 6 7 8/8

Printed in the U.S.A.

For Robbie

Children rarely get the opportunity to speak out on the important issues of our times. After all, they're just kids. They play kickball, watch TV, and eat candy bars. They don't have a care in the world, right? Wrong.

Given the chance to voice their concerns, children show how much they care — and know —about what's going on in the world. SCHOLASTIC NEWS gave children across the U.S. that chance. What they gave back is a powerful plea to society — to listen to their longings and fears about the future. More than 32,000 children in grades 1-6 entered the SCHOLASTIC NEWS Journalism Awards Contest. They wrote essays beginning with the statement, "If I could ask the Presidential candidates one question, I would ask. . . ." The questions they asked, from those about out-of-work parents to others reflecting concern about nuclear war, create a montage of emotions and intelligence that demonstrates an almost frightening awareness.

The questions demand to be heard.

The idea for the contest sprang from a fundamental belief that drives the SCHOLASTIC NEWS staff every day in creating a weekly newspaper for kids: KIDS COUNT. We take children seriously. They are the future caretakers of our world.

Through the contest, children got personally involved in choosing our next President. The questions they asked and their reasons for asking revealed their deepest feelings. "The contest gave me a chance to write about how I feel. I've been worrying about nuclear war for years. The essay came from my heart," the fourth-grade winner, Craig Byrne, told us.

The selected essays in this book include entries submitted by the winners and runners-up — and others we just couldn't leave out. The process of making the selection was a moving experience for all of us at Scholastic. We're proud to be sharing the essays with you.

Helen Benham
Editorial Director
SCHOLASTIC NEWS

Contents

Nuclear War

"Does the rain falling outside my
window have fallout in it?"

Name: John Jones
Age: 6 years
Grade: First
School: Lincoln School
Wausau, Wisconsin

Why Do you make Bombs and why Do you make guns that make wars plese stop the wars.

Name: Jason Aaron Joyce
Age: 7 years
Grade: First
School: Pennell Elementary School
Aston, Pennsylvania

If you were president, would you be willing to start a nuclear war? I knowing that no one could live through a nuclear bombing and there are lots of things I want to do when I grow up.

Name: Stacey Piccinati
Age: 6 years
Grade: First
School: Phoenix Country Day School
Phoenix, Arizona

If I could ask the Presidential candidates one question I would ask, can we have some peace in this world? Because I like peace and quiet because I like to read and create games.

Name: Frank Messana
Age: 7 years
Grade: First
School: Flamingo Elementary School
Davie, Florida

If I could ask the Presidential candidates one question, I would ask, "How are wars started and how can wars be stopped?" I don't like hearing about people being killed or hurt. It's important that the U.S. shows other countries how to live in peace.

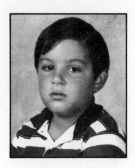

Name: Mark DeLellis
Age: 8 years
Grade: Second
School: Winn Brook Elementary School
Belmont, Massachusetts

If I could ask the presidential candiates o question I
would ask,

Dear candaidates, If you
were President and the world was going to
blowup would you let people have a free
space craft ride to another planet?

This is important because there
might not be life ever again.

Name: Katie Brown
Age: 7 years
Grade: Second
School: St. Isaac Jogues School
Hinsdale, Illinois

If I Could Ask the Presidential candidates one question. I would ask if World peace is really possible. I am 7, but as far I can remember whenever I watch the news thats all that I ever hear about & how the whole world could be blown up. This is very spooky since I want to grow up in a safe & happy world & want the same thing for every one, even people in Russia.

Name: Patrick McCullough
Age: 8 years
Grade: Third
School: St. Joachim's School
Beacon, New York

If I could ask the Presidential Candidates one question, I would ask what strategies they would take to avoid a nuclear war.

Will I have to worry if my milk has that something in it, or will I have to get under my desk in school when a nuclear alarm sounds? Does the rain falling outside my window have fallout in it? Are the planes flying over my house war planes?

Many times I see frightening headlines that two major countries cannot come to an agreement and I ask my parents, are we going to have war?

Name: Rachel Rowley
Age: 9 years
Grade: Third
School: Center School
West Willington, Connecticut

If I could ask the Presidential candidate one question, I would ask...

If your ever president would you let Nuclear War happen? My question is important because I'm still in my early ages. When the lights go out I get scared and my mother always looks out the window. I think there's to many Nuclear missles! I think that we should be able to hold hands and be friends. Bye.

from,
Rachel Rowley

Nuclear War

Name: Anne Ufheil
Age: 9 years
Grade: Third
School: Northwest Elementary School
Huntington, Indiana

If I could ask the Presidential candidates one question, I would ask why we have so many nuclear missiles.

I am afraid that one of your computers will goof up and say that somebody is sending a missile. Then you'll send a few missiles and then the world will blow up because of a computer and a huge stockpile of nuclear weapons.

Name: Terri Wenkman
Age: 8 years
Grade: Third
School: St. John the Baptist Catholic School
Jefferson, Wisconsin

Dear Mr. President,

I am very intersted in owr space program. My question is however, do you feel that owr space program will cause us to to draw nearer to war with the Russians because each side will try to put weapons up there in space to try to have power over the other country? I hope we never have war with erybody. because I want to be a doctor when I grow up.

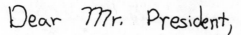

Name: Nickisha Rivera
Age: 9 years
Grade: Third
School: St. Joachim's School
Beacon, New York

If I could ask the Presidential Candidates one question, I would ask why should we have a Nuclear Bomb if its going to destroy every living and human thing on this earth? I like what God gave us on earth. Do you feel its right to destroy a beautiful land that we live on? What will the future be without good soil to plant our seeds?

We children have nothing to look forward to if its to be taken away from us

Nuclear War

Name: Steve McManama
Age: 10 years
Grade: Fourth
School: Stanley Clark School
South Bend, Indiana

"If I could ask the presidental canidates one question I would ask," "Why don't you put a freeze on nuclear arms". We would save billions of dollars a year. And the metal we use for the tube, of a missle we could use for a car". "As for the engines of some guided missles, in which some they are jet engines". The engines could be used for passenger jets". "If the U.S. got into a nuclear war sure it help the economy, it always has, but many innocent Americans world lose thier lives". "People wouldn't have to worry about the economy because there wouldn't be any more people to worry about it". "You might be afraid that the Russians might take over but I'm sure if you talk to them right they might stop building nuclear bombs, also".

Name: Susan Heim
Age: 9 years
Grade: Fourth
School: St. Margaret School
Woodbury Heights, New Jersey

If I could ask the Presidential candidates one question, I would ask:

President Reagan, why he continues to make more nuclear weapons.

I wonder what good it does to make more nuclear weapons when there are already enough to actually destroy the earth. I think it is more important to freeze the numbers of weapons and then start to eliminate them one at a time. I know it will take a very long time, but it must begin sometime. This earth and its people are too important to trust its survival to the hope that somebody, somewhere won't use a nuclear bomb. This is a very real threat because this country has already used atomic bombs in Japan during World War II. So you can't say it will never happen...it already has.

Nuclear War

Name: Craig M. Byrne
Age: 10 years
Grade: Fourth
School: Packanack School
Wayne, New Jersey

If I could ask the Presidential candidates one question, I would ask: " How will your relationship with Russia be? "

The United States and Russia are the most powerful countries in the world. I feel that if the United States and Russia are friends, then a nuclear war is less likely to occur. If there were a nuclear war, there would be no place to hide. The world would be demolished and I would too. I want to grow up, and maybe someday I could be the President.

This question is important to the future of our country, because if the United States, and Russia, could combine their talents in the fields of research and development, they would probably be able to cure diseases that they never imagined they could. Just think how wonderful the world would be with all the talents of the United States and Russia combined!

Name: Sara Jane Gardner
Age: 9 years
Grade: Fourth
School: Asa C. Adams School
Orono, Maine

If I could ask the Presidential candidates one question, I would ask ... If we stopped building nuclear bombs and the Soviet Union didn't stop, would you spend money to build more bombs just to be stronger then the Soviet Union instead of using it for schools, hospitals, and new businesses for the unemployed?

I think we should stop building bombs and use the money for more worthwhile purposes such as hospitals, schools, and charity. If we build more bombs, we might have a disaster on our hands. If the bomb storage area caught on fire accidentally, the United States could be blown up. Other countries don't compete to see who's better. We make fools of ourselves by trying to act big. Why can't we have peace? We might, if you stop building bombs.

Nuclear War

Name: Jessica Presto
Age: 10 years
Grade: Fourth
School: Flanders School
East Lyme, Connecticut

If I could ask the Presidential Candidates one question I would ask, "Would we have a chance against a Nuclear Bomb?"

I would like to know because I would like to live a long life, and I have a lot of good things in my life.

If you would say, "Yes, we would have a chance against a Nuclear Bomb." I would continue to live in Connecticut with my family and friends; but if you would say, "No, we wouldn't have a chance." I would force my family to move away, I mean far away. I can't stop myself from thinking about it.

My neighbor says it is dumb to think about it, but I think it matters.

The End

Name: Erik Boyd
Age: 10 years
Grade: Fifth
School: Moffit School
Springfield, Oregon

"If I could ask the Presidential candidates one question, I would ask, If you are elected as our next President of the United States what qualifications do you and your party have that would make my town and your town "safer from a nuclear war?

I'm concerned that the United States and Russia possess more nuclear weapons than are necessary for national security. Our nation and the Soviet Union are the two major super powers, each trying to out do the other...

I have a friend who has relatives who live in Russia. His uncle came to visit Oregon in 1978. He stayed for one month. He said that people living in Russia are afraid that the United States wants to destroy their country with nuclear weapons. I'm afraid that Russia will destroy us!

If you are elected as our next President I hope you will help prevent a larger build up of more nuclear arms. It scares me and my friends!

Name: Rachel Ellis
Age: 10 years
Grade: Fifth
School: Westwood Elementary School
Friendswood, Texas

Dear Presidential Candiates,

"How are you going to prevent the Nuclear War?"

The reason I would like to know is because I don't want the same thing to happen to me that happened to Sadako Saski. When she was only two years old, the United States dropped the Atom bomb on Hiroshima, Japan—the city she lived in. Ten years later, when she was only 12 years old, she died of leukemia as a result of the radiation. The nuclear bomb is worse, so what will happen to me? I am only ten years old and in the 5th grade. I would like to live to be at least 25 or older.

Name: Aaron Harty
Age: 12 years
Grade: Sixth
School: St. Stephen's School
Merchantville, New Jersey

If I could ask the presidential candidates one question it would be about nuclear war. I don't know why you people keep making missles when you know a couple of them could wipe out the face of the earth. I hope you consider this a serious subject because it is. Why don't we just live in peace and harmony? Why don't the countries cooperate and be happy? I hope you do something about this because I want to live for a pretty long time and I'm sure other people want to live longer. Can't the U.S. and the Soviets work something out to make my life easier?

Name: Mitchell Maltz
Age: 12 years
Grade: Sixth
School: Hebrew Academy
Miami Beach, Florida

Canditates

Will your policies permit me to Survive in this Nuclear age? I am a twelve year old native born Miamian. I recently read were President Reagan returned to his home town of Dixon Ill. after more than 70 years since his birth. Do you think I will be able to also return to my home town after many years? will your nuclear policies prevent this from happening?

Unemployment and the Economy

"Why is my dad having such a hard time finding a job?"

Name: Kristina Feher
Age: 7 years
Grade: First
School: Pennell Elementary School
Aston, Pennsylvania

Would you lower the prices? If you lower the prices it would make life easier for people who don't have lots of money.

Name: Chelsea Russell
Age: 6 years
Grade: First
School: Hickman Run School
Fairmont, West Virginia

Dear Mr. Candidate
Would you
open up all the
closed factories
so my Dad can
make good money
again, like he used
too.

Unemployment and the Economy

Name: Elias Bailey
Age: 7 years
Grade: First
School: Jenkins Elementary School,
Newport News, Virginia

If I could ask the Presidential candidates one question, I would ask, "What do you have in mind to help small businesses?" My mom has a chimney sweeping business called "Mary Poppins". She works very hard and I would like to see something done to help her.

Name: Bridget McKean
Age: 8 years
Grade: Second
School: Gilbert Elementary School
Gilbert, Iowa

If I could ask the presidential candidates one question I would ask. Would you allow the jobless of America to build railroads, parks and other public buildings?

Name: Christopher Raphael
Age: 7 years
Grade: Second
School: Phillippi Shores Elementary School
Sarasota, Florida

If I could ask the Presidential candidates one question, I would ask, "Will there be enough jobs for me and my friends when I grow up?" because we will need jobs to earn money to buy new things. we want to live in a nice house.

Name: Monica Cegelski
Age: 7 years
Grade: Second
School: Holy Trinity School
Pittsburgh, Pennsylvania

If I could ask the presidential candidates one question, I would ask why can't you do something to get the Steel-mills working again? I live where a lot of people are out of work. Many families don't have enough food to eat and may lose their homes.

Name: Karl F. Wittkopf
Age: 8 years
Grade: Second
School: Florence Elementary School
Florence, Wisconsin

If I could ask the presidential candidates one question, I would ask... "Why are the taxes so high?" I think that question is important so we know where our money is going. I don't think that tax money should be spent on bombs that could blow up our country because then I could never grow up to pay taxes.

Unemployment and the Economy

Name: Heather Backhaus
Age: 7 years
Grade: Second
School: Cleveland School
Sioux Falls, South Dakota

IF I could ask the presidental candidate one question, I would ask," Can you lower the food prices?" Too many people go without good food and they can not do their best work without it. Then my mom could save money for my college.

Name: Marcia Powell
Age: 7 years
Grade: Second
School: Hickman Run School
Fairmont, West Virginia

Dear Mr. President.

Will there be more jobs in West Virginia this year?

Why cant more business use coal from our coal fields?

Will the older people have money to buy their needs?

Name: Tracy Miller
Age: 8 years
Grade: Third
School: Bailly School
Chesterton, Indiana

If I could ask the Presidential candidates one question, I would ask if he could give my daddy a job. He is a very hard worker. Also, he'll take any job he can get. He is working now but I never get to see him. He hardly get any money, so please get him a better job!

Name: Chad Phillips
Age: 8½ years
Grade: Third
School: St. Michael's School
Hastings, Nebraska

If I could ask the Presidential Candidates one question I would ask...... Why are the prices of products going up? I need to know becuse when I get older I want to get a fair price on food, clothing and all other butiful stuff like football helmets and basketballs uniforms hats, and footballs and basketball hoops.

Unemployment and the Economy

Name: Jimmy Clark
Age: 8 years
Grade: Third
School: Pleasant Lea Elementary School
Lee's Summit, Missouri

Dear Mr. Candidate,
If I could ask the presidential candidate one question I would ask, "Why does there have to be such a thing as money?" Because then people wouldn't have to worry about being kicked out of their homes and not being able to pay their rent, and other things like that.

Unemployment and the Economy

Name: Michael James McClain
Age: 9 years
Grade: Fourth
School: St. Rosalia School
Pittsburgh, Pennsylvania

If I was able to ask the presidential candidates one question, I would ask, why are we sending so much money all around the world to help other people, when right here in our own country the United States we have:

1. High unemployment,

2. Children and people that are hungry,

3. Men looking for jobs that can,t be found,

4. Old people that can,t live off of Social Security,

5. People that can,t pay their gas or light bills,

6. Familys losing their homes due to no income and

7. People waiting in lines for food.

I feel my question is important because, I feel the people in the United States needs as much help if not more than people in other countrys. My answer is important because I feel the government of the United States should help it,s country first.

Unemployment and the Economy

Name: Stacey L. Arnold
Age: 9 years
Grade: Fourth
School: Benton Elementary School
Wichita, Kansas

The reason I'm asking this question is because many of my friends' parents have been layed-off and millions of other people get layed off each year. When unemployment is stopped everybody will be happier and if the people are happier then the crime rate will most likely be lower than it has been for years! If people have jobs then they don't need to rob for money to support their families.

Name: Jennifer Troyer
Age: 9 years
Grade: Fourth
School: Bernita Hughes Elementary School
Adair, Oklahoma

If I could ask the presidental candidates one question, I would ask what could you about the problems facing farmers such as high interest rates rising form expenses and low milk prices?

This is important to me because I am a nine year old girl and I live on a small dairy farm. Its hard to make ends meet We don't want to have to sell out. We wouldn't like to see small family farms replaced by large companies. How would you solve this problem?

Name: Jesse Dellen
Age: 11 years
Grade: Fifth
School: St. Peter's School
Columbia, Pennsylvania

If I could ask the Presidential candidates one question, I would ask, "What will happen to people without jobs?"

The Answer to this question is important to the future of the United States because with all the new machines in the world, it's taking less people to run them. Soon no one will have jobs to support their families. Prices will go up and make it harder. Then people will not have money to buy food or gas. The amount of people will go down because they can't buy medicine or pay the doctor's bill. That is why I think something should be done about it

Name: Nathan Scott
Age: 11 years
Grade: Fifth
School: S.D. Spady School
Delray Beach, Florida

If I could ask the Presidential canidates one question, I would ask, "How will you provide work for all those who want to work?"

I would ask this question because if people had jobs, and money for his or her family, they wouldn't have to go out and steal and deceive for money.

A second reason I would ask this question is because many people in our community are commiting suicide and all starting to use drugs, because they think their lives are worthless.

The finale reason I would ask this question is because

people are being thrown out into the street because they can't pay their bills and dying of hunger, sickness, and cold.

If people had jobs, there would be enough welfare for the elderly and disabled; they're the ones who really need welfare.

I thought this question was important because, if people had jobs, there would not be so much hatred, deceits, stealing, murder, and muggings. If it was like that, the U.S. would be a nicer place to live in.

Unemployment and the Economy

Name: Stephan Weber
Age: 11 years
Grade: Fifth
School: Alexis I. Dupont Middle School
Wilmington, Delaware

If I could ask the Presidential candidates one question, I would ask this. Everyone claims that the condition of the country is improving. If this is so, why is my dad having such a hard time finding a job? My dad has been out of work for seven months. He has been trying very hard to find work somewhere but has had no luck. What are you planning on doing to improve the conditions of our country? If you do become President, what will you do to increase the number of jobs in our country so that my dad will be able to get a job? It is not very much fun living on such a tight budget as we have been doing. I know there are lots of other families who are in our same situation. They will all be very interested in your answer.

Unemployment and the Economy

Name: Angela Edwards
Age: 11 years
Grade: Sixth
School: St. Michael's School
Schererville, Indiana

If I could ask the Presidential candidates one question, I would ask what they would do to improve unemployment rate. I would ask this question because if many more factories shut down too many people would be out of jobs. People with less money would buy imported goods because they are cheaper. Soon other factories would close down in America because of poor business, and more people would be out of jobs. And our trade would be cut down.

In Chicago, they closed down Wisconsin Steel Works, that put hundreds of people out of jobs, including my uncle. And now, on March 1 they are closing General Mills down. My father is plant manager of a flour mill. For the third time, we have to move away from my family. People are getting so crazy about this, that someone called and said there was a bomb in the plant. It isn't fair. And I think we should do something about it!

Unemployment and the Economy

Name: Jenny Crosswhite
Age: 11 years
Grade: Sixth
School: Sheridan Middle School
Sheridan, Arkansas

If I could ask the Presidential candidates one question I would ask, "Can my parents afford to send me to college?"

I will go to college six years from now. Six years ago the University of Arkansas cost an average of $1,250 yearly. Now it costs $3,580 yearly. How much will it cost six years from now when I am ready to go?

What I want to know is, "Will my parent's salary keep pace with inflation sufficiently to send me to college?"

I think this is important because many students won't be able to go to college if their parents can't afford to send them. I'm one of them. I make good grades, and always take part in school activities. I'm sure there are many students like me. We are the leaders of tomorrow. The quality of our leadership depends on education.

Helping the Needy

"Will you promise that no one will be hungry in America?"

Helping the Needy

Name: Chris Seliga
Age: 7 years
Grade: First
School: Holy Rosary School
Kenosha, Wisconsin

Winner Grade One

If I could ask The presidential candidates one question I would ask How will you help old people when They get sick? It is important That we help old people because They worked for our country to make it better for us.

Name: Jonathan Harvey
Age: 6½ years
Grade: First
School: Henry C. Lea School
Philadelphia, Pennsylvania

If I could ask the presidential candidates one question, I would ask: When you're president will you solve our problems like people who go with out heat, electricity, or water? My question is important because people who go with out heat, electricity, or water might become extinct. And then there will be no world.

Name: Shawn Campbell
Age: 7 years
Grade: Second
School: Hattie Cotton Elementary School
Nashville, Tennessee

If I could ask the presidential candidates one question, I would ask him Would you please build houses for the poor? Because many, people are suffering and dont have houses to live in.

Name: Michelle Purkapile
Age: 8 years
Grade: Second
School: LeRoy Elementary School
LeRoy, Minnesota

"If I could ask the presidential candidates one question I would ask, would you help the poor because the whole world is filled with poor people, I think they should have vegetables, milk and steak

Name: Peter DeMik
Age: 8 years
Grade: Third
School: Our Savior Lutheran School
Arlington, Virginia

If I could ask the Presidential Candidates one question I would ask: What will we do with the poor people? I feel bad that they don't have the money to buy things like toilets and running water and good food. We need to give them a chance of getting better education so that someday the people who are poor now will be walking out the door of a shiny marble house.

Helping the Needy

Name: Tanéha Friend
Age: 8 years
Grade: Third
School: Barron School
Hampton, Virginia

Winner Grade Three

Mr. Candidate,

If you were elected president would you increase or decrease the funds for the space program?

We spend billions of dollars on space programs but we have forgotten our fellow man here in the U.S.

On the news I saw people eating out of trash cans and sleeping on benches.

I feel we should spend more money on the needy and less on space program.

Name: Amy Walker
Age: 9 years
Grade: Third
School: St. Anselm School
Brooklyn, New York

If I Could Ask the Presidentail Candelates One Question I would Ask.

Mr. President would you be able to make homes for the homeless? Every day when I go to school there is a bum named Elmer Fud. He has no home or family. It would be so nice If he had a place to go. He has a black and blue head. It always bleeds. Another bum I know is called Rob the bum. He is nice to me. He is like a person. These men should not have to sleep on my street. Can you help them?

Helping the Needy

Name: Nathan Morris
Age: 8 years
Grade: Third
School: Whiteside School
Belleville, Illinois

If I could ask the presidential candidates one question, I would ask: Is hunger a real problem In America?

Many people in our country are starving today, especially in big cities. We transport food and money to other countries, but we have hunger here. Some wealthy presidential candidates do not realize the real problem of starvation in America. For America to be truly great, we must feed our own.

Name: Keira McGovern
Age: 8½ years
Grade: Third
School: Brookside School
Brookfield, Wisconsin

If I could ask the presidential candidates one question, I would ask what programs would you make to educate the poor. If they don't get enough education we could miss out on a good leader-someone that is interested in politics and who would like to be our president.

Name: Staci Ross
Age: 9 years
Grade: Third
School: Roose School
Warren, Michigan

"If I could ask the Presidential candidates one question, I would ask If you become President will you promise that no one will be hungrey in America? Because there are so many children, babies and older people are dying from hungar and that realy makes me sad and mad. I like people that care.

Name: Johanna Deuchler
Age: 10 years
Grade: Fourth
School: Our Lady of Good Counsel School
Aurora, Illinois

I think you should find ways to use farm surplus products more wisely. An investigation should be made to decide if outdated but still nutritious grocery store food items could safely be used to feed the hungry. I think there should be stricter rules to decide who can get free food so that the truly needy will be better fed.

Name: Scott Walker
Age: 9 years
Grade: Fourth
School: St. Jude the Apostle School
Atlanta, Georgia

If I could ask the presidential candidates one question I would ask. "What do you feel should be done about all the poor people?"

I feel each person should have a place to live and some clothes to wear. There are a lot of people in the United States who are dying from starvatoin and no place to sleep on cold nights. I think this is important because I feel it is the duty of all people to help all people who are in need.

I think this is important in the future as populatain increases it will be even more important to see that each one has the necessary means to live

Helping the Needy

Name: Mia Harper
Age: 11 years
Grade: Fifth
School: Lomond School
Shaker Heights, Ohio

If I could ask the Presidential candidates one question, I would ask, "What do you plan to do with the Senior Citizen situation?" The Golden Agers face many crisises. Many don't have enough money for food transportation, medical bills. They live fearful lives due to crime in the cities They cry at night and moan during the daylight hours.

My grandmother is 72 years old. We call her "Nama". Everbody in our neighborhood loves her. I'm glad she lives with us so that we can look out for her. But what can you promise to do about the others who have no one and are very lonely? Will you commit yourselves to the aged.?!

Name: John Burch
Age: 12 years
Grade: Sixth
School: St. Joseph's School
Mechanicsburg, Pennsylvania

Dear Sirs:

If I could ask the Presidental Candidates one question, it would be this:

"HOW ARE WE EVER GOING TO MAKE ENDS MEET IN THE UNITED STATES?"

Everything you read in the newspapers or see on television has to do with the state of the economy. People don't have jobs or any income to pay for the common necessities of life. There are so many people who can't afford food, and they have to receive free cheese and some canned goods and milk to live on.

No one should have to live like this. You live well and have a nice home and plenty of food to eat whenever you want it.

Please tell me how you will help all the people in the United States of America have more prosperity and less poverty.

Thank you.

Helping the Needy

Name: Michael Po
Age: 11 years
Grade: Sixth
School: Public School 178
Jamaica, New York

If I could ask the Presidential candidates one question, I would ask "Why? Why are we worrying about constructing hotels and building gigantic space stations that cost millions of dollars when there are so many needy and hungry, homeless people in the United States!"

I understand that we once in a while, give out free cheese and butter but couldn't we give more attention to these poor people? This is important to the future of our country because if all of our streets were clean, and nobody was lying around, starving, homeless, and cold, and if these people got an education, think of how our country could grow! These people who were once poor might become great scientists, scholars, and maybe even the President of a country! Please, give more attention to the needy of our country.

Name: Alicia Boldreghini
Age: 11 years
Grade: Sixth
School: St. Mary's Catholic School
Jackson, Tennessee

"If I could ask the presidential candidates one question I would ask about the children of the united states who are very poor or who are not treated right. Some kids of the u.s.a. have lives to live but sometimes when people do not have enough money they think there is no hope. So do the kids, so they lead awful lives. These children need help; so do their parents. They need jobs and money so they can put these children in schools so they will grow up and be good citizens of the united states. The reason I write about this + why it would be good for the U.S.A. is these children want to grow up and lead normal lives :)

P.S. The reason I did not write about nuclear arms is I am sure you get too many letters like that a day anyway :)

The Environment

"How are you going to keep
the air I breathe safe so that
I can grow up?"

Name: Ryan Dedmon
Age: 6½ years
Grade: First
School: Bright Horizons School
Carrollton, Texas

If I could ask the Presidential candidates one question, I would ask how are you going to keep the food I eat and the air I breathe safe and healthy so that I can grow up?

Name: Josh Stuart
Age: 6 years
Grade: First
School: Quailwood School
Bakersfield, California

If I could ask the Presidential candidates one question, I would ask could we have laws about keeping our country clean? If there is litter all over it might catch fire.

The Environment

Name: Jennifer Grandpre
Age: 6 years
Grade: First
School: Wakelee School
Wolcott, Connecticut

If I could the Presidetia candidates one question I would ask that there would be no more water pollution. I would ark that question so all the water animals wouldnat

die out. Some of the animals are almost extinct. I want the crodile and alligator to stay alive so they could be the longest living creatures on Earth!

Name: David Johnson
Age: 7 years
Grade: Second
School: Atwater School
Shorewood, Wisconsin

What would you do to stop people from throwing things on the ground ? We need to keep our country Clean.

Name: Adam Kitzen
Age: 8 years
Grade: Second
School: Woodward Parkway School
Farmingdale, New York

This year in Farmingdale there was a week or two when we couldn't drink the water.
It was polluted. There were dirty things in the water and people were getting sick. Many people had stomach aches.
We couldn't drink water in school or at home. Our moms had to go out and buy bottled water.
It was scary.
What if it happened again to the whole country? What can you do to make sure this doesn't happen?

Name: Emily Turner
Age: 8 years
Grade: Second
School: Prairie View School
Eden Prairie, Minnesota

If I could ask the presidential candidates one question I would ask " Why does there have to be so many roads? Why can't there be any country around. we should have country because cities make too much noise. They stink. There are too many roads and too many houses They are tearing down fields just to make roads and houses.

Name: Tami Haydocy
Age: 8½ years
Grade: Third
School: Dorothy Lewis Elementary School
Solon, Ohio

If I could ask the presidential candidates one question I would ask why don't they stop making cigarettes because it would help in keeping the United States have clean air.

The Environment

Name: Sarah Lock
Age: 8 years
Grade: Third
School: Lockhart Primary School
Lockhart, Texas

If I could ask the Presedential candidates one question would ask........ How should people save endangered species?

Some animals are becoming rarer and rarer. I am determined to save those animals. When I grow up I'm starting a group to save them. I'm going to do better than they are doing now. I really want to save them.

Name: Andrew Hargarten
Age: 8 years
Grade: Third
School: St. James School
Mequon, Wisconsin

If I could ask the Presidential candidates one question, I would ask are you going to make more rules about protecting animals and their homes? Because someday, maybe the only animals alive will be mice, rats, other rodents, and insects. That's if something isn't done. Some people think it's better to look fancy than it is to have the world look pretty.

The Environment

Name: Torri Taylor
Age: 9 years
Grade: Fourth
School: Irmo Elementary School
Irmo, South Carolina

If I could ask the Presidential candidates one question I would ask If you were elected what would you do to help stop pollution? This is an important question because if the air and water are polluted how can people and animals drink and breathe? It's very important to our future because if pollution gets worse the whole world could die. All the plants would fall down dead and so would we. Then there would be no more world.

Name: Robby Hall
Age: 11 years
Grade: Fifth
School: Hunt School
Sioux City, Iowa

If I could ask the Presidential candidates one question, I would ask—"How will you prevent water and air pollution so it will not kill living things, like birds that fly in the air?" If we stopped polluting water and stopped the smoke from big factories, then the birds and the fish could live happier lives.

I think this question is important because the birds in the sky and the fish in the rivers and animals that drink from the rivers can be killed if the pollution is strong enough and then we will no longer be able to enjoy them.

The Environment

Name: Diane Noll
Age: 11 years
Grade: Sixth
School: Blessed Sacrament School
Fort Mitchell, Kentucky

If I could ask the presidential candidates one question, I would ask if pollution is an important issue in their presidential platform, and what they're going to do to improve our environment?

I think this is an important issue because I live in Northern Kentucky, and when I drive through the industrial areas of Cincinnati I can see the thick smoke coming out of the smookstacks. It sickens me to think I'm breathing in the polluted air. The smell makes me want to hold my nose or just not breathe at all. On the news they say that carbon dioxide is making our temperatures higher. I know It won't affect me, but in 100 years or so if pollution is still going on the temperatures will be so hot that it'll be just like we're living on the equator and it'll be very uncomfortable. I hope that in 100 years we'll be able to say our ~~enviro~~ environment has improved.

Name: Tracy Lynne Mertens
Age: 11 years
Grade: Sixth
School: St. Thomas More School
Bethel Park, Pennsylvania

If I could ask the presidential candidates one question, it would be: What would you do as the President to safely clean the radio-active sights in the United Sates? The reason why I would ask this question is because I had to change schools because there was too much radio-active waste at the school I used to attend. During the last half of my fourth grade year at this school, I had to wear a radiation badge. I don't think that it is a very good idea for young children at that age to have to think about wearing a badge or about the effects of radiation.

Other reasons that I think that this is a problem are that many people have lost or will lose their houses that they have invested in. Some people who are exposed to radio-active wastes have gotten sick and many more people will probably get sick too. Most of these illnesses have been some form of cancer. I think that cleaning these sights safely would add to the well being of many people.

Education

"Will you put more money into education?"

Name: Kortney Tambara
Age: 6 years
Grade: First
School: C.J. Morris Elementary School
Walnut, California

If I could ask the Presidential candidates one question, I would ask them if they could give a little more money to the schools because we need to learn alot about differnt things so that when we grow up we will be able to help our country keep peace.

Name: Bradley Kessler
Age: 8 years
Grade: Second
School: Padan Elementary School
Vacaville, California

If I could ask the presidential candidates one question, I would ask, Would it be possible to have more computers in the Classrooms? Computers help children Learn. Computers help teach children things they need to know. Computers Let children Learn at their own pace.

Education

Name: Mark Medeiros
Age: 8 years
Grade: Second
School: A.S. Letourneau School
Fall River, Massachusetts

If I could ask the Presdential candidates one question, I would ask them if they would hire some people to fix some of the schools in the United states. My reason for this question is that some of the schools need new paint jobs, new chairs, and new desks.

Name: Matt Shanks
Age: 8 years
Grade: Third
School: Bailly School
Chesterton, Indiana

If I could ask the Presidential Candidates one question I would ask them if they think school years and days should be longer. I wouln't really like them to be longer, but it might give us more time to learn more things. My question is imporant to the country because we need to learn more.

Name: Beth Cackowski
Age: 8 years
Grade: Third
School: Warnsdorfer School
East Brunswick, New Jersey

If I could ask the Presidental candidates one question, I would ask

What can we do to help our schools teach children better?

It has been found that children are not being taught as well as they could be. Something must be done to improve the way that the basic subjects are taught in our schools especiaely in the cities.

Education

Name: Brian Clarence Strait
Age: 9 years
Grade: Fourth
School: Crawford Elementary School
Crawford, Nebraska

If I could ask the Presidential Candidates one question, I would ask why they don't upgrade the education level?

Schools in the United States are falling behind schools in other countries. For example, we had an exchange student from Sweden living in our home. He graduated from our school but had to take his senior year over because it was not accepted in his country.

Who should pay for the education? Should states and towns pay for it? Some people think the federal government is not giving enough money for education.

Education is so important to me because if I am not well-educated I will not be able to get a good job when I grow up. In the news we keep hearing that our education level is falling.

What are you going to do about it?

Name: Dominic Thompson, Jr.
Age: 9 years
Grade: Fourth
School: Seven Holy Founders School
Affton, Missouri

"If I could ask the Presidential candidates one question, I would ask, what are you going to do for public and private education if elected?"

I believe that this question is the most important thing facing America today. The future of our country is going to be in the hands of kids like me. We can not be expected to face the challenges of tomorrow without getting the best education possible. Money for both private and public education should be very important to our future president. If the president thought it was really important, then our governor would too. Teachers salaries have to get better, so that good teachers like the ones I have now, will keep on being teachers. The future Presidential candidates of tomorrow, maybe even myself, are being educated today. And as my parents often say, "You only get what you pay for."

Education

Name: Darcy Janes
Age: 10 years
Grade: Fourth
School: Clark Elementary School
Le Mars, Iowa

If I could ask the Presidential candidate one question, I would ask...."Why spend money for making nuclear weapons when you can use the money to help schools?" Spending money for nuclear would get us in a nuclear war with other people. If you use less money for nuclear weapons and use more for schools we would have more and better schools and better books. Use less money for nuclear weapons to fight with. Otherwise we would die. In the future if we could have better schools, teachers, books, materials, we could learn more how to stop fighting and learn more about our Presidents if we did.

Name: Dennis Kalian
Age: 10 years
Grade: Fifth
School: Public School 28
Yonkers, New York

If I could ask the Presidential Candidates one question I would ask "What do you plan to do to help make our educational system better?"

I think we should have better programs especially in science and math. These more intensified programs will help us in future technology. There should be more enrichment centers for the gifted and talented that offer classes five days a week. I think all American children should learn a foreign language as early as Kindergarten so that by seventh grade they'll be quite fluent in it. There should be more computers and more computer classes. This is important because our country is in a high technology stage. All these things are important to our children because we are the future of our country.

Name: Trey-Bo Heath
Age: 11 years
Grade: Sixth
School: St. Paul's Episcopal School
Winter Haven, Florida

If I could ask the Presidental Canidates one question I would ask, "How are you going to help the educational system in the United States?"

This question is important because our educational system is getting lower in quality and the school programs have been cut twenty-five percent. Why are we lagging behind many European and Asian Countries? I think this question will be useful in the future because we could have better quality schools and better education. Politicians <u>must</u> know that great scientists and inventors are in proportion to the quality of the educational system.

Crime

"Why do people steal?"

Name: Christy McCoy
Age: 6 years
Grade: First
School: Quailwood School
Bakersfield, California

If I could ask the Presidential candidates one question, I would ask what can we do about people who take other people's things? You need to be able to keep the things that are important to you.

Name: Aviva Krauss
Age: 7 years
Grade: Second
School: Bais Yakkov School
Kew Gardens, New York

If I could ask the Presidential candidates one question I would ask Why do people steal? I am asking this because if stealing doesn't stop, some people will not have anything to live on.

Name: Tanya Griffith
Age: 7 years
Grade: Second
School: Northern Parkway Elementary School
Uniondale, New York

If I could ask the Presidential candidates one question I would ask if he could prevent drunk driving because people are getting other people in accidents. And More people are dying from accidents.

If he could stop that it would mean so much to me. So please make a law saying Stop! Drunk Driving. So people could understand that drinking is not good for you.

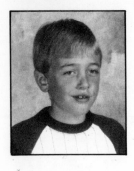

Name: Joseph Thierry
Age: 9 years
Grade: Third
School: Our Savior Lutheran School
Arlington, Virginia

If I could ask the presidential candidates one question, I would ask why we can't take guns or other weapons away from all the people.

This is important to the future of our nation because then less people could get killed. If people want to hunt then they could rent guns.

Name: Michelle Brodzik
Age: 10 years
Grade: Fourth
School: St. Thomas Grade School
Crystal Lake, Illinois

If I could ask the Presidential canidates one question, I would ask them, What would they do concering the drug abuse situation in our schools today? As a ten year old student I am really worried about all I hear, about how kids my age are being sold drugs and alcohol right in our schools. What can be done to keep children from falling victim to these people who push drugs? Also what would you do to help prevent other children from selling drugs to their classmates? Would you push for stronger laws to stop the sale of illegal drugs and alcohol to minors? It's terrible, the things that these drugs do to children's bodies and minds, and often killing them. I really feel that something very drastic should be done and also that no time sould be wasted.

Name: Alison Shurpin
Age: 9 years
Grade: Fourth
School: Abraham Joshua Heschel Day School
Northridge, California

If I could ask the Presidential candidates one question, I would ask "How can you stop crime?". I think this is a very important problem because a lot of people are getting mugged, robbed and molested. Even poor people are innocent victims. My house has been robbed three times in one year. One time the robber smashed the bedroom window. I think there should be a way to stop crime. I know one way you could stop it. The way I think you can stop crime is to have a worse penalty for crime, but not death. Maybe the penalty should be a longer time in jail, longer than robbers are jailed now. I hope you feel the same way because I think this is a very important problem. I also hope you can stop it. Please consider my idea.

Thank you,

Name: Tara Grove
Age: 10 years
Grade: Fifth
School: St. Peter's School
Columbia, Pennsylvania

If I could ask the Presidental candidates one question I would ask, "What are you going to do about all the missing children of the world?"

The answer to this question is important to the future of the United States, because children are being kidnapped from their own neighborhood. You see all those children on television reported missing. You can't even go into a shopping mall without hearing about a child being kidnapped from the shopping cart. People are going around in shopping malls and taking five year olds and younger children into the bathroom and shaving their hair. Then they try to leave the store with the child. The people who kidnap these kids either sell them or kill them.

Crime

Name: Richard Luna
Age: 11 years
Grade: Sixth
School: Saints Felicitas and Perpetua School
San Marino, California

If I could ask the Presidential candiates one question, I would ask what they are going to do about the use of guns by people. I would like to know how they would stop the selling of guns. I feel this is important because my father is an officer of the law. And it scares me to know that somebody's out there in this country who has a gun that in one shot could kill my father. I would like to know if they are worried about being shot by a person with a gun.

Name: Susan Petring
Age: 12 years
Grade: Sixth
School: Kearny Elementary School
Santa Fe, New Mexico

If I could ask the Presidential candidates one question, I would ask, "What do you plan to do to reduce crime in the United States?"

The answer to this question is important for the following reasons:

1. People are living in fear and locking themselves in their own homes and essentially becoming prisoners in their own homes. This is denying Americans one basic freedom to come and go as they please.

2. Crime is costing Americans a tremendous amount of money. If this is allowed to continue unchecked, it could have a devastating effect on the economy.

3. If criminals are allowed to continue operating, they can only gain more power, including political power, which could eventually destroy our democratic system and our free society.

Equal Rights

"Are women allowed to be President?"

Name: Matthew Ramos
Age: 6 years
Grade: First
School: Quailwood School
Bakersfield, California

If I could ask the Presidential candidates one question, I would ask how can we help each other be equal? People feel bad when they are not treated the same.

Name: Jennifer Bosshardt
Age: 7 years
Grade: Second
School: St. Charles School
Kansas City, Missouri

If I could ask the presidential candidates a question I would ask, "Are women allowed to be president?" This is important because men have been president for 200 years. Some people are tired of men presidents and want women presidents.

Name: Bridget Sullivan
Age: 8 years
Grade: Second
School: St. Mary's School
Niles, Michigan

Winner
Grade
Two

If I could ask the Presidential candidates one question I would ask.... What do you think of a lady president? It would be new — different. We must think of everyone in a land that is free.

Name: Lisa Doyle
Age: 9 years
Grade: Third
School: Lockhart Primary School
Lockhart, Texas

If I could ask the Presidential candidates one question, I would ask, "Would you require females to serve in the military if there was a war?"

I think there are lots of females who would like to know if they might have to do military service. If females are to ever do military service, I think some sort of training needs to be started for them now so they will be prepared.

Name: Lauren Edelman
Age: 10 years
Grade: Fifth
School: St. Joseph Hill School
Staten Island, New York

If I could ask a presidential candidate one question it would be what he plans to do about equal rights for women. My reasons are that men think women can't do anything they can do. I, for one, know that when I grow up, I would want to get a chance at good jobs like men get. We also shouldn't have to be housewives. Women should be able to be mechanics or house builders, just like men. Men think we shouldn't do it because we'll get dirty, but most women don't care about that. Men just don't know that because they don't even give us a chance. And that would be my question I would ask a presidential candidate.

Equal Rights

Name: Yu Wong
Age: 11 years
Grade: Sixth
School: Public School 61
New York, New York

If I could ask the Presidental candidates one question, I would ask the position they take on the "Equal Right amendment." This particular question interests me because it has been a controversy ever since the 1840's. Women have been considered lower than the men. for thousands of years. They ask only for equal rights. They ask only to be treated the same as the men. This question is very important to the future of America for many reasons. One reason is that women have taken an important part in American history. For example Lydia Darragh who warned the American troops at White marsh of an attack by the British in the Revolutionary war. Another reason is that women are very important to the future of the world. I think that women will one day gain equalty with men. They are skilleful and smart. One day America will need them One day the world will need them.

Name: Amy Kitchen
Age: 11 years
Grade: Sixth
School: Graebner Elementary School
Sterling Heights, Michigan

If I could ask the Presidential Candidates one question, it would be: What will you do to help people gain all their rights in America?

I think all people should respect others for what they are. Noone should judge people by their skin, race, sex, or what they look like.

When I went to buy my Cabbage Patch Kid, they only had black ones left. I thought they were cute, but some people didn't. One mother said she wouldn't buy one for her daughter, or let her daughter buy it herself, because "it was a waste of money." I bought one.

People ask me why I bought a black one. They act like the doll is inferior because she has darker skin. I realized how prejudiced people could be.

The President must work to stop prejudice. The President must protect the right of all people. I think people are the most important ingredient to make our country great!

Presidential Leadership

"What makes you special enough
to be the leader of our country?"

Name: Elisabeth Weinstein
Age: 6 years
Grade: First
School: Solomon Schechter Day School
Baltimore, Maryland

If I could ask the Presidential candidates one question, I woud ask... Will you be honest about every thing that you say? I hope so. If a person makes a promise they should keep it. Presidents shouldn't lie.

Name: Bridget Miller
Age: 6 years
Grade: First
School: Solomon Schechter Day School
Newton, Massachusetts

If I could ask the Presidential candidates one question, I would ask, "How do you want people to remember you after you are President? We learned about Abe Lincoln. People remember what a great man he was."

Name: Elana Weisband
Age: 6 years
Grade: First
School: Memphis Hebrew Academy
Memphis, Tennessee

If I could ask Presidential candidates, one question I would ask why did you want to be a president? What makes you special enough to be the leader of our country?

Name: Andy Ross
Age: 7 years
Grade: Second
School: Glasco Grade School
Glasco, Kansas

If I cuold ask the Presidentil candidates one question I would ask Why are their speechs so long? My question is important because If the candidates talk too long people won't listen. If they don't listen they won't know what you stand for.

Name: John Roberts
Age: 8 years
Grade: Second
School: Memorial School
Milford, Massachusetts

If I could ask the Presidential candidates one question, I would ask if $200,000 a year is a lot for a President. Maybe you should share it with your gardner, your body guards, help pay your chauffeur's gas bill.

Name: Jennifer Rathsack
Age: 8 years
Grade: Third
School: Johnson Elementary School
Golden, Colorado

If I could ask the presidential candidates one question, I would ask when the president has a pile of papers on his desk, when does he have enough time to read them all in a certain hour.? I think this question is important because some stores, or different states might send very important letters for the president to read and answer.

Name: Rachelle Smith
Age: 9 years
Grade: Fourth
School: Bates Academy
Detroit, Michigan

If I could ask the Presidential candidate one question, I would ask him why did he choose to run for President because some people just run for President because they want more money and more FAME. Other people run for President because they want to help to put an end to all the confusion in our country. They are concerned about missing children, rape and killings. They are also worried about our position in the world and stability at home. They want to cut prices, end unemployment and help to make the poor a little richer. I would like to ask the candidate to tell me the honest truth, "Which person are you??"

Presidential Leadership

Name: Matt Richmond
Age: 9 years
Grade: Fourth
School: Mercer School
Shaker Heights, Ohio

If I could ask the presidential candidates one question, I would ask, "Do you think that one six-year term in office for the President of the United States would be preferable to the two four-year terms now allowed?"

It seems to me that the President has to spend a lot of time thinking about getting re-elected for his second term instead of thinking about the country. If the President didn't have to spend so much time organizing the campaign, travelling around the country and learning campaign speeches, he could be concentrating on nuclear disarmament, the economy and unemployment, U.S. involvement in trouble spots like Lebanon and World Peace.

Name: Sheri Kubaszewski
Age: 10 years
Grade: Fifth
School: W.A. Driscoll School
Centerville, Ohio

Many presidents have had a slogan or saying that they can be identified with. For example, Franklin D. Roosevelt said "the only thing we have to fear is fear itself." John F. Kenedy said "ask not what your country can do for you, but what you can do for your country." If you would choose a slogan or saying that would best represent what you stand for, what would it be, and why?

Presidential Leadership

Name: Jeff Riddle
Age: 12 years
Grade: Sixth
School: Concord East Side Elementary School
Elkhart, Indiana

Winner Grade Six

If I could ask the Presidential candidates one question, I would ask the following: If it were possible to ask advice from any three people from history that admire for the purpose of helping to solve problems of today, who would you ask and what questions would you ask?

I think this question would give me insight into the candidates' character. You can tell alot about a person from knowing who that person respects and admires. Our country needs to have public officials elected to office who have good character. Hearing the questions the candidates would ask would give me information about what they feel are important issues to the future of our country. I believe this question reveals what is in a person's heart, not just what he says in speeches.

Special Subjects

"Who invented love?"

Name: Monica Gavinski
Age: 6 years
Grade: First
School: Lincoln School
Wausau, Wisconsin

Can you fix my moms Car Whae Can you do it I am asking you this question to see if you know how

Name: Bradley Friedman
Age: 6 years
Grade: First
School: Solomon Schechter Day School
Baltimore, Maryland

If I could ask the Presidential candidates one question, I would ask, " If Martians attack the worlds would the United State and Russia fight them together?" It is important for them to fight Martians together, because if they don't, they won't ever have a chace again.

Name: Nathan Koch
Age: 7 years
Grade: First
School: Heuvelton Central School
Heuvelton, New York

If I could ask The Presidential candidates one question, I would ask "What would you do in the hear future for space exploration?"

If we didn't explore space we wouldn't know much about it. If he said no, there would be no more space exploration.

Name: Jon Nagel
Age: 6 years
Grade: First
School: Horizon School
Tampa, Florida

If I could ask the presi- dential candidates one question, I would ask who invented Electricity. Because I use Electricity for my things and my clock

Name: Todd Caltabiano
Age: 8 years
Grade: Second
School: Mickleton School
Mickleton, New Jersey

what are you going to do about Valcanos erupting? Do you know that many lives were lost because of Valcanos erupting?

Name: Jasper Kennedy
Age: 6 years
Grade: First
School: Horizon School
Tampa, Florida

If I could ask the Presidential candidates one question I would ask who invented life. I would ask because I want to know how they did it.

Name: Eric Rachner
Age: 8 years
Grade: Second
School: Brandywood Elementary School
Wilmington, Delaware

I would like to ask how many machines you have; (if you have any). And how they work; (if you have any).

Name: Jaime Archer
Age: 8 years
Grade: Third
School: Indian Grove School
Mount Prospect, Illinois

My question is why don't we have Children's Day? I want Children's Day because mothers and fathers have Mother's Day and Father's Day and children don't have their very own special day. Mothers and fathers feel wanted. Some poor children who don't have any mothers or fathers or don't have any clothes or food could have it on this special day. Some people could go to poor children, to love them and take care of them, give them clothes and give them food. It would make it more special with this day.

Name: Shannon Sysk
Age: 7 years
Grade: Second
School: Horizon School
Tampa, Florida

If I could ask the Presidential Candidates one question I would ask who I invented love.

Because I do not know and I would like to know.